WARREN G. HARDING

ENCYCLOPEDIA
of PRESIDENTS

Warren G. Harding

Twenty-Ninth President of the United States

By Linda R. Wade

Consultant: Charles Abele, Ph.D.
Social Studies Instructor
Chicago Public School System

CHILDRENS PRESS®
CHICAGO

President and Mrs. Harding, photographed in 1923

Library of Congress Cataloging-in-Publication Data

Wade, Linda R.
  Warren G. Harding / by Linda R. Wade.
      p.   cm. — (Encyclopedia of presidents)
  Includes index.
  Summary: Examines the life and career of the Ohio
newspaperman who became the twenty-ninth president of the
United States.
  ISBN 0-516-01368-8
  1. Harding, Warren G. (Warren Gamaliel), 1865-1923—
Juvenile literature. 2. Presidents—United States—
Biography—Juvenile literature. 3. United States—Politics
and government—1921-1923—Juvenile literature.
I. Title. II. Series.
E786.W3   1989
973.91'4'0924—dc19   88-38057
[B]   CIP
[92]   AC

Picture Acknowledgments

AP/Wide World Photos—4, 6, 8 (top 2 pictures),
30 (2 pictures), 31 (bottom), 36, 38, 57, 60, 65
(top), 72 (2 pictures), 73 (top), 75 (top), 83
(top), 89

Historical Pictures Service, Chicago—5, 8
(bottom), 9, 16, 18 (2 pictures), 21, 24, 27, 32,
33 (2 pictures), 34, 35 (2 pictures), 37, 44 (2
pictures), 45 (2 pictures), 46, 47, 49 (bottom),
52, 58, 59 (3 pictures), 62 (bottom), 65
(bottom), 67, 68, 69 (3 pictures), 73 (bottom),
77, 78, 85

Library of Congress—49 (top), 74 (bottom)

North Wind Picture Archives—28, 29, 82

Lindaanne Donohoe, illustrator—15

UPI/Bettmann Newsphotos—10, 12, 26, 31
(top), 41, 43 (2 pictures), 50, 51, 53 (2 pictures),
54, 62 (top), 63 (2 pictures), 74 (top), 75
(bottom), 79, 80, 83 (bottom), 86, 87, 88

U.S. Bureau of Printing and Engraving—2

Cover design and illustration
by Steven Gaston Dobson

The Presidential Peace Medal
commemorating the inauguration
of Warren G. Harding in 1921

Table of Contents

Chapter 1

Masked Friends

Warren G. Harding was a man who could not say no to his friends, and his friends became his downfall. Some of them were more interested in getting rich than in doing a good job for their country. Some went so far as to make illegal deals that brought a black cloud over Harding's administration.

News of these scandals began to leak out in 1923, a few months before the president's death. More wrongdoing was uncovered in the months following his death. Two government officials even committed suicide because they could not face being caught and punished for their crimes.

Charles R. Forbes, head of the Veterans' Bureau and one of Harding's friends, went on trial for bribery and conspiracy. In the "Teapot Dome" affair, Secretary of the Interior Albert Fall made several hundred thousand dollars in a crooked deal with two oil companies. Harding's close friend, Attorney General Harry Daugherty, stood trial twice for conspiring to defraud the government.

Above: Secretary of the Interior Albert B. Fall (left), known for his involvement in the "Teapot Dome" oil scandal, and Attorney General Harry Daugherty (right), tried for selling government favors

Left: A 1923 political cartoon showing the difficulties of victims of a housing shortage during Harding's administration

Secretary of Commerce Herbert Hoover

Warren Harding died before these scandals were made public. He never knew how badly his name would be blackened by the corrupt activities of his friends. Though he himself was not involved in the scandals, his administration is remembered for its corruptions.

Harding made the mistake of appointing people to important government posts simply because they were his friends, not because they were qualified. Perhaps he was not a strong leader, and the terrific responsibility of being president was more than he could handle alone. One thing is certain: He was eventually betrayed by his friends.

Herbert Hoover, who was Harding's secretary of commerce, later said: "Harding has been betrayed by a few men whom he had trusted, by men who, he believed, were his devoted friends."

Chapter 2

Early Years

In the little village of Corsica, Ohio (now known as Blooming Grove), Warren Gamaliel Bancroft Winnipeg Harding was born on November 2, 1865. Only seven months before, the Civil War had come to a close with the surrender of the last Confederate troops. Times were hard for the country.

Warren's parents had known each other for many years. The Hardings and the Dickersons lived on neighboring farms, and George Tryon Harding and Phoebe Dickerson were schoolmates and sweethearts in the days just before the Civil War. When the war broke out, George entered the Union army and became a drummer. Upon his return, he built a little house on his father's farm and married Phoebe. Warren was the oldest of their eight children.

The boy's young father was a farmer who supplemented his income as the village physician. Phoebe cared for all the children. She also took special training to become a professional midwife, delivering babies.

Harding's birthplace in Corsica, Ohio

Warren was called "Winnie" while he was very young. He was a fast learner and loved to sit at his mother's knee. She taught him the alphabet by writing with a stick of charred wood on the bottom of a shoebox. She also taught him poems before he was four years old. Her encouragement made him confident that he could succeed in whatever he did.

When Warren was ten years old, his family moved to the village of Caledonia. There he attended a school and was good at spelling and at writing essays. As he walked to school, he sometimes found Indian relics along the way.

Warren grew tall and strong and enjoyed all sports. He often played baseball with his schoolmates. Though he had a prankish nature, he made lots of friends.

At home, Warren helped the growing family by cutting trees, chopping wood, splitting rails, and planting corn. He also had a cow to milk every morning and evening and a stable to keep clean. One of his chores was to curry (clean and brush) Doctor Harding's team of horses after he returned from his daily house calls.

Warren was ambitious and eager to earn money. When he was only ten, a farmer near Caledonia found himself short of men to cut corn. Young Harding agreed to help, and by the end of one long week he had earned six dollars.

His father also gave him a chance to earn a few dollars. He plowed half an acre of land for Warren to plant in wheat. The boy harvested eighteen bushels, took it to the warehouse at a nearby village, and received eighteen dollars.

Later the Toledo & Ohio Central Railroad was laying new track about a mile east of the Harding place. When Warren finished his farm chores, he worked for the railroad with a team of horses for four dollars a day.

Warren's father had become part owner of the village newspaper, the *Caledonia Argus*. There Warren learned to set type and worked as a "printer's devil," or messenger and office boy.

Young Harding loved music and obtained a secondhand B-flat cornet. Often he practiced into the night in order to master new music. He joined the city band and enjoyed playing at park concerts.

At the age of fourteen he entered Ohio Central College, an academy in Iberia, Ohio. He paid his tuition of seven dollars per term, plus living expenses. Occasionally he had to quit his classes and go back home to earn additional money.

Warren gained such a reputation for painting barns that he was in great demand. He and a friend "literally painted the county red," wrote one biographer. When asked about his prices, Harding would reply, "Two dollars each-a-day 'till we finish, or $25 for the whole job—we furnish the paint."

Of course, the time that it took to paint a barn depended on which agreement had been made.

Warren became editor of the school newspaper, the *Ohio Central College Journal of Knowledge and Josh*. This opportunity became a determining factor in his career. Interested in people, he read at least ten biographies a month. He also took a deep interest in government and took pride in the fact that he could name many senators and governors.

In 1882, Doctor Harding moved his family once more, this time to Marion, Ohio. After graduating from Ohio Central that same year with a bachelor of science degree, Warren journeyed to his new home. There he passed an examination that allowed him to teach.

He accepted a job teaching in a one-room schoolhouse for a term, but was not happy being a teacher. He studied law for a short time, but found this too tedious. Next he tried selling insurance. Finally, in 1883, Warren turned to journalism.

Harding as a schoolteacher in Ohio

Chapter 3

From Printer to Politician

Warren Harding's newspaper career began in 1883, when he applied for a job at the *Marion Mirror*. For seven dollars a week he scrubbed floors, sold advertisements, delivered papers, secured interviews, and wrote editorials.

Warren had grown up in a home that usually followed the Republican point of view. Now he became very interested in politics and went to Chicago to attend his first national Republican convention. There James G. Blaine was nominated to run as the presidential candidate and John A. Logan was chosen as his running mate. Harding was proud to be a Republican and obtained a campaign hat with BLAINE-LOGAN printed in bold letters across the headband.

When he returned to Marion, his boss, who was a strong Democrat, told him to write an article attacking Blaine. Warren refused. In fact, he defiantly appeared at the office the next morning in his Blaine hat. Either the hat or the job had to go, the boss informed Harding. Warren chose to wear the hat.

Above: 1884 Republican presidential candidate James G. Blaine
Below: A ticket to the 1884 Republican National Convention

Now unemployed, he turned to music, which not only provided personal enjoyment but gave him a weekly income.

"I played every instrument but the slide trombone and the E-flat cornet," Warren remembered.

"I once took the Marion band to Findlay," he reported. "We had no uniforms and we couldn't appear without them. So I borrowed money to pay for the uniforms by persuading a local merchant to endorse the bank note. I believed the band would win the prize, but not everyone shared my belief. In order to gain complete cooperation I had to guarantee one man his wages and pay the doctor bill for another one. But I got the band to Findlay, in uniform, and we won the prize."

He laughed. "This money helped me buy the Star."

One night in 1884, Warren walked into a restaurant on Marion's Main Street. There he met two of his friends, and they began discussing the small Marion newspaper that was for sale.

"Let's buy the Star!" Harding suggested. So with only $300, the three of them went into business. One man soon dropped out, so Jack Warwick and Warren Harding then found themselves co-owners of the *Marion Star*. Harding was only nineteen years old.

Warren loved the oily odor of printer's ink and anything associated with the newspaper office. He became an expert at setting type by hand. When a typesetting machine called the Linotype was first introduced, he learned to operate that, too. He was proud to call himself a practical tradesman in the newspaper business.

The *Star* was a struggling daily paper, but the young editor had great enthusiasm, inspiration, and determination. Sometimes he worked far into the night. Warren's mother had a quiet confidence in her oldest son. While the paper was struggling she told Jack Warwick, "You and Warren will make a success of the Star."

Whenever possible, Harding kept unpleasant stories out of the paper. He wanted to be an agreeable neighbor, and he wanted to avoid making things any harder for men "whose weaknesses got them into trouble." Warren had no patience with some newspapers' tendencies toward sensationalism at that time. He said, "I believe if I were to write a code and could write it for all the newspapers of America, I would ban anything of a vicious character except that which is necessary as a public warning."

The town of Marion grew and so did the *Star*. New churches and neighborhoods, a music hall, and many new businesses appeared. All of these were noted in the *Star.*

His office was on the second floor of an old building in the center of town. Each morning Harding walked to work, stopping to greet people by their first names. He asked about their families and showed interest in their problems. Soon the townspeople began to call him "W. G." By the time he was twenty-five, Harding's newspaper had become quite a success.

It was about this time that he met Florence Kling. She was the daughter of Amos Kling, a wealthy Marion businessman. Florence, five years older than Warren, was divorced and the mother of a young son. In addition to raising her child, she taught piano lessons. Florence and

The office and printing plant of the *Marion Star*

Warren started dating and soon became engaged. From the beginning she called Harding "my Warren," and he gave her the stately title of "the Duchess."

The couple chose a nice location in Marion and built their home at 380 Mount Vernon Avenue. It was to this home that they invited a few close friends and were married in the parlor on July 8, 1891.

Florence soon became an active part of the *Star*. "I went to the office to help out for a few days," she remembered, "and stayed for fourteen years." As manager of circulation, Florence trained a crew of newspaper delivery boys. She ran the business portion of the *Star* and Warren handled the news writing and printing. While not as softhearted as Warren, Florence was highly respected. Together, their efforts made the *Star* a popular newspaper.

The Star Office Creed

Remember there are two sides to every question. Get Both.

Be truthful.

Get the facts. Mistakes are inevitable, but strive for accuracy. I would rather have one story exactly right than a hundred half wrong.

Be decent. Be fair. Be generous.

Boost—don't knock. There's good in everybody. Bring out the good in everybody, and never needlessly hurt the feelings of anybody.

In reporting a political gathering, get the facts; tell the story as it is, not as you would like to have it.

Treat all parties alike. If there's any politics to be played, we will play it in our editorial columns.

Treat all religious matters reverently.

If it can possibly be avoided, never bring ignominy to an innocent woman or child in telling of the misdeeds or misfortune of a relative. Don't wait to be asked, but do it without asking.

And, above all, be clean. Never let a dirty word or suggestive story get into type.

I want this paper so conducted that it can go into any home without destroying the innocence of any child.

Warren G. Harding
Editor & Publisher of the *Marion Star*

The set of rules that Harding posted for his employees to follow as they prepared their news stories for the *Marion Star*

Warren was mechanically skilled and could repair any press breakdown. Also, he loved words and enjoyed writing the editorials. He understood the laboring man, sympathized with the newspaper labor union, and always carried his union membership card with him. Warren developed a profit-sharing plan that gave his employees at the *Star* not only their salaries but also a share of the paper's profits.

Warren wrote a set of rules and had them posted in full view of all employees and visitors. The rules encouraged fairness, accuracy, and decency. As much as possible, these ideas were carried in every article. They became known as "The Star Office Creed."

Soon new columns were added, and national and world news came in by the Associated Press wire service. The *Star* published farm and market reports as well as price information. Warren followed sports, especially baseball, and listed the scores.

The paper prospered and so did the Hardings. They were among the first people in town to own an automobile. They also began to take yearly vacations in the South.

Warren Harding increased his business interests, and his style of public speaking caught the attention of audiences. These factors, combined with his appealing personality, brought him into the public eye. Many people regarded "W. G." as a true friend. He loved the city of Marion, for he had watched and helped it develop from a farm community.

Warren continued to follow politics, backing Republican candidates. His close friends began suggesting that he run for a political office. When a seat opened in the state senate in 1898, they encouraged him to enter the race. At the age of thirty-four, Warren Harding was narrowly elected a member of the Ohio General Assemblies from the Thirteenth District.

Warren Gamaliel Bancroft Winnipeg Harding—known as "Winnie" for a short time, "Warren" through his youth, and "W. G." as a successful newspaperman—had now climbed another rung on his ladder of accomplishments. He had officially entered the political arena.

23

Chapter 4

Climbing the Political Ladder

Almost immediately, Warren Harding became the center of attention in the capital city of Columbus. People began to see the patience, poise, and earnestness that had characterized him throughout his life. As an Ohio state senator he supported Republican policies and widened his circle of friends. His good nature and personality made him well liked by everybody, regardless of party. After winning reelection to a second term, Harding was chosen to be the Republican floor leader, or spokesman, of the Ohio senate.

William McKinley, also from Ohio, had been president of the United States since 1897. McKinley had been elected governor of Ohio in 1891 and reelected in 1893. Warren admired McKinley and sometimes thought of himself as following in McKinley's footsteps.

In 1903, Republican Myron T. Herrick was elected governor of the state of Ohio, with the largest majority in the history of the state. Warren was elected lieutenant governor on the same ticket. After his term ended in 1905, he returned to Marion and gave his attention to the Harding Publishing Company, as his enterprise was known now.

Opposite page: Harding around 1900,
when he was beginning his political career

William Howard Taft

Harding was out of office by his own choice, but he kept up his interest in politics. In 1910 Warren ran for the office of governor of Ohio but lost. Hurt by the defeat, he stated publicly that he would abandon politics and return to journalism. But by 1912, he was actively supporting Republican president William Howard Taft for renomination and reelection. (Taft eventually lost the election to Democrat Woodrow Wilson.)

Early in 1914 some Republicans suggested that Harding would be a good candidate for the United States Senate. Harding hesitated to seek the position, but as sentiment in his favor grew, he allowed his name to be put in nomination. He won not only the nomination, but the general election as well.

Now Harding went to Washington as a senator from Ohio. He made no attempt to make himself conspicuous, but his large and handsome figure and face attracted the attention of visitors in the galleries. Because of his pleasing voice and impressive manner, people listened more carefully to his speeches than to those of many older and better-known senators.

Personally, Harding was liked by political foes as well as friends. He often played golf and attended baseball games with his friends in Washington. Poker had been one of his favorite pastimes while in Marion, and Harding now found senators ready and anxious to gather around the card table.

By the middle of his second year, he was generally recognized as one of the most influential members of the Senate. His membership in the Committee on Foreign Affairs brought him additional recognition.

Senator Harding introduced 132 bills during his six years in the Senate, though none of them was particularly significant. They concerned such matters as securing back pensions for veterans, encouraging the teaching of Spanish, celebrating the Pilgrims' landing, lending surplus government tents to the public during a housing shortage, and investigating influenza.

Since he did not like controversy, he was absent when many controversial matters were being voted upon. In fact, he missed more than 46 percent of the roll call votes during his years in the Senate.

Generally Harding voted with the majority of the Republicans in the Senate. He supported the interests of American workingmen. He also wanted to restore the American Merchant Marine to its former commanding rank on the high seas. He voted for amendments to the Constitution that provided for women's voting rights and prohibition of alcohol.

After the outbreak of World War I in 1914, Senator Harding often supported Democratic president Woodrow Wilson in his efforts to keep America out of war. This war had seemed far away until Germany torpedoed the British ship *Lusitania* in 1915, killing 128 Americans.

In June 1916, Harding was chosen to deliver the keynote speech at the Republican national convention in Chicago. Much of this speech was devoted to the war. He pushed for a strong national defense and encouraged American patriotism, which he called Americanism. "Americanism begins at home and radiates abroad," he declared. He told the delegates that they must take care of

America, for "it is good to be an American." His speech thrust him into the political arena even more.

In January 1917, the British intercepted a message on its way from Germany to Mexico. Germany wanted Mexico as an ally in case of war with the United States. The Germans promised to help Mexico recover land that the United States had taken in 1848. Besides this, Germany had sunk a record number of merchant ships. Finally, on April 6, 1917, the United States declared war on Germany. The Allies then included Belgium, France, Great Britain, Italy, and the United States. On the other side were the Central Powers—Germany, Austria-Hungary, Bulgaria, and the Ottoman Empire (now Turkey).

The nation seemed to join together for the war effort. Even Harding, a staunch Republican, publicly commended Democrat Wilson. Among the wartime measures Harding supported were the Selective Service Act, which called for a military draft to raise a large army; the Espionage Act, which dealt with German spies and disloyal Americans; and the Food Control Act, which enabled America to supply food to the Allies. Harding also backed a bill prohibiting trade with the enemy, a bill for taking over enemy ships in U.S. ports, and the War Risk Insurance bill.

Meanwhile, battles raged in Europe. Finally, in the fall of 1918, the Central Powers surrendered one by one until only Germany remained at war. Many German soldiers and sailors revolted and in the end forced Germany to sign an armistice. The fighting finally stopped on all battle fronts at 11:00 A.M. on November 11, 1918. World War I had ended.

Above: President Wilson asks Congress to declare war on Germany.
Below: America's 126th Infantry on the battle front in World War I

**Above: One tank explodes as another crashes through barbed wire in Flanders, Belgium.
Below: Men of the U.S. 165th Infantry on their way to trenches in St. Clement, France**

EXTRA **The Chicago Daily Tribune.** **FINAL EDITION**

THE WORLD'S GREATEST NEWSPAPER

VOLUME LXXVII—NO. 270. C.   MONDAY, NOVEMBER 11, 1918.—22 PAGES.   * * PRICE TWO CENTS.

GREAT WAR ENDS

Washington, D. C., Nov. 11, 3 A. M. (By Associated Press.)—Armistice terms have been signed by Germany, the State department announced at 2:45 o'clock this morning.

The world war will end this morning at 6 o'clock, Washington time, 11 o'clock Paris time. The armistice was signed by the German representatives at midnight.

USE WIRELESS TO GIVE WORD TO SIGN TRUCE

Germany Uses Nearly All of 72 Hours of Grace.

BULLETIN.
Washington, D. C., Nov. 11, 3 a. m.—The momentous news that the armistice had been signed was telephoned to the White House for transmission to the president a few minutes before it was given to the newspaper correspondents. Later it was said there would be no statement from the White House at this time.

Washington, D. C., Nov. 11, 3 a. m.—There was no information available here this morning as to the circumstances under which the armistice terms were agreed, but since the German courier did not reach American military headquarters until 10 o'clock yesterday (Sunday) morning French time, it was generally assumed here that the German envoys within the French lines had been instructed by wireless to sign the terms.

It is supposed the power which gave to the German emissaries the authority to sign was centered in Chancellor Ebert.

Two Days' Trip of Courier.

Forty-seven hours had been required for the courier to reach German headquarters and an unmistakably several hours were necessary for the examination of the terms and a decision. It was regarded as likely, however, that the decision may have been made at Berlin and instructions transmitted from there by the German government.

Germany had been given until 11 o'clock this morning, French time, 6 o'clock Washington time, to accept. So hostilities will end at the hour set by Marshal Foch for a decision by Germany for peace or for continuation of the war.

Offer Courier an Airplane.

LONDON, Nov. 10.—(British Wireless Service.)—The German

(Continued on page 4, column 1.)

OUTLINE OF THE TERMS
(UNOFFICIAL)

Washington, D. C., Nov. 11.—(By the Associated Press.—(The terms of the armistice, it was announced, will not be made public until later. Military men here, however, regard it as certain that they include:

Immediate retirement of the German military forces from France, Belgium, and Alsace-Lorraine.

Disarming and demobilization of the German armies.

Occupation by the allied and American forces of such strategic points in Germany as will make impossible a renewal of hostilities.

Delivery of part of the German high seas fleet and a certain number of submarines to the allied and American naval forces.

Disarmament of all other German warships under supervision of the allied and American navies which will guard them.

Occupation of the principal German naval bases by sea forces of the victorious nations.

Release of allied and American soldiers, sailors, and civilians held prisoner in Germany without such reciprocal action by the associated governments.

SALUTE POLAND, NEW REPUBLIC!

AMSTERDAM, Saturday, Nov. 9.—A message from Cracow announces the proclamation of a Polish republic under the presidency of Deputy Daszynsky.

Sovereignty Over Galicia.

AMSTERDAM, Nov. 10.—Prof. Lambach, the Austrian premier, has confirmed the official confirmation, sent a dispatch from Vienna, that Poland has acknowledged sovereignty over Galicia.

Galicia is a crown land of Austria-Hungary north of the Carpathians. It has an area of 30,307 square miles and a normal population of about 8,000,000.

Chicago Gets Out of Bed; Bedlam Reigns in Loop

The first taste of the signing of the armistice reached THE TRIBUNE office at 1:58 o'clock this morning. It came in a flash from the Associated Press by telephone. The text of the flash was simply:

"Armistice signed." The Associated Press operator then lined up the chain. By this time the manager flash. By this time the manager of the Associated Press had been in three sections here and others, as usual. The first on the street, telling the people that the hour of democracy throughout the earth had arrived.

In less than thirty minutes from the time the first flash reached the Oke the Loop rang out in a Loop was crowded with the "Peace extra" being sold by newsboys on busy corners.

THE TRIBUNE siren was quickly followed on the request to spread over the city from scores of busses and police station whistles.

First on the Street.

THE TRIBUNE notified the police and fire departments' headquarters. Instantly the memers was relayed to every engine house and police station in the city.

Five Day Jolts Habit.

THE TRIBUNE notified the police and the departments' headquarters. Instantly the memers was relayed to every engine house and police station in the city.

"The new government has taken charge of the administration to preserve the German people from civil war and famine and to

(Continued on page 2, column 6.)

THE WEATHER.

[illegible weather table]

REPUBLIC SET UP IN BERLIN BY SOCIALISTS

Manifesto Pledges Government of and for the People.

BERLIN, Saturday, Nov. 9.—(German Wireless to London, Nov. 10, 12:56 p. m.)—By the Associated Press—The German people's government has been instituted in the greater part of Berlin. The garrisons have gone over to the government.

The Workmen's and Soldiers' council has declared a general strike. Troops and machine guns have been placed at the disposal of the council.

Ebert Tells of Plans.

Friedrich Ebert (vice president of the Social Democratic party) is carrying on the chancellorship.

The text of the statement issued by the people's government reads:

"In the course of the November of Saturday the formation of a new German people's government was initiated. The greater part of the Berlin garrison and other troops stationed there temporarily went over to the new government.

Refuse to Shoot People.

"The leaders of the deputations of the Social Democratic party declared that they would not shoot against the people. They said they would, in accord with the people's government, intercede in favor of the maintenance of order.

"The business of the imperial being carried on by the Social Democratic deputy, Herr Ebert.

"It is presumed that, apart from the representatives of the recent majority group, three independent Social Democrats will enter the future government."

Proclamation by Ebert.

In a proclamation to the people the new German chancellor, Friedrich Ebert, says:

"Citizens: The ex-chancellor, Prince Max of Baden, in agreement with all the secretaries of state, has handed over to me the task of liquidating his affairs as chancellor.

Asks for Help of All.

"The new government has taken charge of the administration to preserve the German people from civil war and famine and to

(Continued on page 4, column 4.)

Kaiser Flees With Staff to Holland

LONDON, Nov. 11, 12:31 a. m.—A party including the former German emperor and also, it is believed, Field Marshal von Hindenburg, arrived at Eysden, on the Dutch frontier, at 7:30 o'clock Sunday morning, according to Daily Mail service.

That party's correspondent at The Hague says the Dutch government has ordered the ex-kaiser and his party interned.

According to another report, the former emperor's eldest son, Frederick William, deposed crown prince, crossed the Dutch frontier with his father.

Practically the whole German army and two automobiles carried the party, the Daily Mail report continues.

The automobiles were bristling with rifles and all the fugitives were armed.

Smokes a Cigaret.

The ex-kaiser was in uniform. He alighted at the Eysden station and paced the platform, smoking a cigaret. Eysden lies about midway between Liege and Maastricht, on the Dutch border.

The emperor entered the staff, the former emperor, the swine stream, and brought back a second train, in which were a large number of staff officers and others and also an escort.

The German arrived from Maastricht and some hours ago, when Dutch railway officials soon made their appearance and many of the inhabitants came to the station attracted by curiosity.

Many photographs were taken by the people of the imperial party. On the whole the people were very quiet, but the Belgians among them yelled out "En voyage!"

HEADED FOR CASTLE.

Washington, D. C., Nov. 11—William Hohenzollern arrived this morning in Holland and is proceeding to Middachten castle, in the town of De Steeg, according to a dispatch received by the American army general staff from The Hague based on press reports in the Netherlands capital.

The dispatch, dated today, said:

"Press reports state that the kaiser arrived this morning at Maastricht, Holland, and is proceeding to Middachten castle, in the town of De Steeg, near Arnheim."

Twelve Miles from Border.

De Steeg is on the Guelders Yssel, an arm of the Rhine river, about four miles east of Dieren and twelve miles from the German border. The Chateau Middachten, to which the former emperor is reported to be proceeding, lies in the town of De Steeg, near Maastricht. Chateau Henry von Bismarck.

BOTH SIGN "DOWN."

Now William signed a letter of abdication and the Emperor Charles of Austria-Hungary yesterday signed one of like nature and the two men placed themselves in the care of the Crown Prince Frederick William of Prussia and the Archduke Joseph of Austria.

(Continued on page 4, column 5.)

RED FLAG FLIES OVER ALL BIG GERMAN CITIES

Rebels Continue to Gain; May Exile All Kings.

LONDON, Nov. 10.—With the Social Democratic party leaders and soldiers' and workmen's councils in full control in Berlin, the revolution in Germany is extending rapidly, according to Amsterdam and Copenhagen dispatches.

In most places the desired effect is being achieved without violence or serious disorders.

"Little Bloodshed in Berlin."

An official dispatch received by the Havas agency from Berlin today says:

"Official. The revolution has resulted in a striking victory almost without the effusion of blood.

"A general strike was declared this morning. It brought a cessation of work in all workshops about 10 o'clock.

Troops Join Rebels.

"A regiment of Nuremberg chasseurs passed over to the people. Other troops rapidly followed their action.

The Alexander regiment, after hearing a declaration by Deputy Wells, went over to the revolution."

Complaints already have been heard in Berlin that the press censorship is being exercised as arbitrarily by the news as by the old regime.

Reports from Germany describe the revolt on as continuing quietly in the twelve principal towns and ports, which are now ruled by the soviet, consisting of workmen, soldiers, and sailors.

Against All Kings.

The Socialists, according to the report, are demanding that every dynasty in Germany be suppressed and all the princes exiled. It is reported that the kings of Bavaria and Saxony intend to abdicate shortly.

The population in the south German states are delighted that German rulers are obliged to seek the abdication of the kaiser.

There has been public rejoicing near the Swiss frontier and also in Alsace-Lorraine.

Red Flag Over Palace.

The red flag has been hoisted everywhere. It is flying above the royal palace in Berlin and from the Brandenburg gate. It can

(Continued on page 4, column 6.)

KRUPP WORKS' CHIEF AND HIS WIFE ARRESTED

LONDON, Nov. 10—(2:18 p. m.)—Essen, where the great Krupp steel works are situated, is reported to be on the hands of the revolutionists, says a dispatch from Amsterdam to the Exchange Telegraph company. Later, Krupp von Bohlen und Halbach, the head of the Krupp works, and his wife, formerly Bertha Krupp, have been arrested. This news was brought from Essen by Dutch workmen arriving for special train at Zevenaar on Saturday.

Leipzic Joins Revolution.

COPENHAGEN, Nov. 10—Leipzic, the largest city in Saxony, has joined the revolution.

A council of workmen and soldiers has been established at Chemnitz, Saxony, according to the Wolff News agency. The council took charge of military and civil affairs. There were no disturbances.

Wurttemberg Joins Revolt.

BASEL, Switzerland, Nov. 10—Wilhelm II., the reigning king of the new kingdom of Wurttemberg, abdicated on Friday night.

Stuttgart, the capital of Wurttemberg, has joined the revolution.

The soldiers' councils at Stuttgart, Cologne and Frankfort have decided to proclaim a republic.

Rebels Hold Luebeck.

COPENHAGEN, Nov. 10—The Rostock Volkszeitung of Saxon announces that Form, the capital of the grand duchy of Mecklenburg-Schwerin, also has been revolutionized and that both civilians and military have been shot.

Rebels Hold Big Cities.

LONDON, Nov. 10—Cologne, on the Rhine, is completely under the revolutionary domination by Prussian city, one in the hardest of the military forces. Many persons, both civilians and military, have been shot.

A train filled with soldiers has been sent out from Bremen for the purpose of persuading other towns to join the revolution.

has been placed above the cathedral in Cologne.

The soldiers and workmens councils on most of the large cities appear to be devoting their efforts to organizing the food supplies, foreseeing that any lack of provision in this regard will produce a fruitful source of disorder.

Some Princes Help.

In some places, notably in Anhalt, Hesse-Darmstadt, and Mecklenburg-Schwerin, the princely houses are co-operating with the workmen in establishing a new order of things.

The burgomaster of Berlin and the prefect of police have placed themselves and their staffs at the disposal of the new government.

More Big Cities Rebel.

Among the latest towns to join

(Continued on page 4, column 7.)

A newspaper announcement of the armistice and German surrender

**Above: Workers at New York's Broadway and Fulton streets celebrating the war's end
Below: Victory parade in Washington, D.C., in 1919**

President Wilson is cheered by Europeans after the end of the war.

Differences between President Wilson's policies and the Republican senator's views began to surface now. When Wilson insisted that the peace treaty be coupled with the formation of a new League of Nations, Harding opposed Wilson. He said that a peace treaty should be made first and a League of Nations considered later. Harding's major objection was over Article Ten of the league's covenant. This article said that, at any time, the U.S. Army and Navy could be sent to take part in a war in which this country had no interest. Instead, Harding called for a voluntary association of nations to settle disputes on the basis of international law. This difference would become a major issue between the Democrats and the Republicans in the 1920 presidential campaign.

Above: The "Big Four" who negotiated the Versailles peace treaty after World War I: (Left to right) David Lloyd George (England), Vittorio Orlando (Italy), Georges Clemenceau (France), and Wilson.   Below: The 1920 Republican national convention

Harry Daugherty, Harding's friend, manager, and later attorney general

When the Republican national convention met in Chicago during the summer of 1920, Harding was not considered one of the front-runners to receive the nomination for president. However, after four ballots the convention was deadlocked over General Leonard Wood and Illinois governor Frank O. Lowden. Both men had roughly equal support among the convention delegates.

That night, powerful Republicans met in a "smoke-filled room" in the Blackstone Hotel. There Harry Daugherty, Harding's friend and campaign manager, suggested Harding's name as a compromise candidate. When his name was introduced at the convention the next day,

Harding around the time of his nomination for the presidency

the delegates remembered the man who had been a friend to all. They had heard his challenge to America and knew of his love for his country. In one speech he had coined a new phrase. He had said that the country needed a "return to normalcy." The delegates began to feel that Harding could present hope to a country tired of war and rising prices. Yes, Harding could carry the Republican banner to victory.

Finally, on the tenth ballot, his nomination was confirmed. The Republican party made an official call to Warren Gamaliel Harding in Marion, Ohio: "Will you be our candidate and lead the country 'back to normalcy'?"

Chapter 5

Campaigning—
Front Porch Style

When the call went to Mr. Harding, the city of Marion began to celebrate. Newspaper accounts said that the big whistles in the Marion Steam Shovel Factory sounded the call of celebration. They roared like an ocean liner. Every electric light post on East Center Street was adorned with a cluster of flags.

Senator Harding chose to remain in his hometown and conduct a "front porch" campaign. His porch was already large, and a portico was added to act as a platform. From here the future president met and talked with dignitaries, co-workers, friends, and neighbors. Candidate Harding was a first-rate handshaker and charmed the people who came by train to meet him.

Harding's neighbor, George B. Christian, Jr., permitted his home to become the staff headquarters. A press house was built behind the Harding home with a wood-plank walk leading to the door. The press liked Warren Harding and gave accurate accounts of his speeches. Occasionally, they were given copies even before the talk was delivered.

Opposite page: Harding campaigning
from his front porch in Marion, Ohio

On July 22, 1920, Harding gave a speech officially accepting his nomination. In it he set forth the principles that would guide his campaign and presidency. He expressed his belief in "America first" and in "a great human brotherhood." . . . "More than all else," he said, "the present-day world needs understanding."

He encouraged competition in business and called for understanding between employers and employees. He supported agriculture and praised farmers, saying, "The American farmer had a hundred and twenty millions to feed in the home market, and heard the cry of the world for food." He also praised the men and women who had served the country through the war.

He promoted a strong budget system. He wanted to expand world trade, have good military branches, and do away with child labor. If elected president, Harding wanted to re-establish a good relationship with Mexico. He also stressed law enforcement.

Near the end, Harding looked into the faces of his followers: "Have confidence in the Republic! America will go on. . . . I pledge fidelity to our country and to God, and accept the nomination of the Republican Party for the Presidency of the United States."

Applause sounded, not only from the city of Marion, but also from a nation anxious to find answers. Now it was time to meet the people as a presidential candidate. This would be a historic election, for it was the first one in which women could vote.

Warren Harding opened his "front porch campaign" on Saturday, July 31, with a homey talk to 2,000 factory

A front porch
campaign speech
before a crowd
of visitors

workers, businessmen, and farmers. Between then and
September 25, some 600,000 persons flocked to Marion
and listened to the Republican candidate. He spoke to visit-
ing groups about the issues that affected them. He
regarded them as his neighbors and seemed to get close to
the American people in these heart-to-heart talks.

Telegrams poured in. Between 200 and 1,000 were read
daily. Mail came in bags.

Marion was a railroad center, and visitors came by train from all parts of the nation. Improved roads also made the Ohio city easy to visit. People were anxious to shake hands with Senator Harding. Warren liked this contact, and his firm grip gave people a sense of security. "It's the most pleasant thing I do," he once told a neighbor.

Bands came to serenade Warren, and they listened as he told them of his days playing the cornet. Glee clubs sang to him while he smiled and tapped his foot. He listened to popular singer Al Jolson's campaign song:

> We think the country's ready
> For another man like Teddy.
> We need another Lincoln
> To do the country's thinkin'.
>
> Mis-ter Har-ding,
> You're the man for us!

Mrs. Harding took an active part in the campaign and was especially appealing to the women voters. She loved the crowds, the full days, the excitement, the speeches, and the parades. She was always the perfect hostess, even when thousands of feet tramped down her shrubs and flowers. In a note to her friend Evalyn McLean, she wrote, "No matter what comes into my life I shall always regard this summer as one of the greatest epochs."

Harding enjoyed talking about patriotism, or Americanism, saying our goals must be: "To safeguard America first, to stabilize America first, to prosper America first, to think of America first, to exalt America first, to live for and revere America first."

Above: Harding takes a turn with the Marion town band.
Below: Warren and Florence Harding in their garden

Top: An anti-Harding
cartoon making fun
of his "America First"
campaign slogan

Bottom: A 1920 cartoon
on the woman's vote.
Its caption reads,
"Will she be a more
careful shopper than
her husband was?"
(The 1920 election
was the first in
which women could
vote for president.)

Top: A 1920 cartoon showing Republicans and Democrats rushing to get the votes of America's 25,000,000 women voters

Bottom: A 1920 cartoon captioned, "It's the little things that count"—showing the "little things" as the American voters

Democrat James Cox (right) with Franklin D. Roosevelt (elected president in 1932)

On many controversial issues, Harding took the Republican party's position. By taking no definite stand, he hoped to bring unity back to the Republican party. The party had been severely split at the Republican convention when the two leading candidates, General Leonard Wood and Governor Frank O. Lowden, were unable to collect a winning number of delegates.

By stressing Americanism, Harding offered hope to people who were tired of war and opposed to President Wilson's policies. Ohio governor James M. Cox, the Democratic nominee for president, supported many of Wilson's ideas. Harding spoke against Wilson's League of Nations proposal. Instead, he was in favor of an "association of nations."

A 1920 cartoon showing
a sentimental version
of Harding's plea for
a "return to normalcy"

In total, Harding gave forty speeches from his huge front porch on Mount Vernon Avenue. He was a quiet gentleman and a conciliator, and he never called his opponent by name. He stressed party unity and wanted to be known as a man who consulted rather than commanded.

Senator Harding's campaign plan also included some extensive travel. He gave speeches in several cities. A railroad tour took him to New York and back through the four big cities of Ohio: Cleveland, Akron, Cincinnati, and Columbus. With its large population, Ohio would be critical in winning the election.

Soon the time came for the people to vote. Did they want to continue with the Wilson policies, or did they want to get back to normal?

Election day in 1920 was Warren Harding's fifty-fifth birthday. After a small celebration, the Republican candidate, his father, his wife, and his campaign manager, Harry Daugherty, listened to the early election returns. This was the nation's first presidential election to be covered by radio broadcast.

Doctor Harding remained until about 10:00 P.M., when it had become obvious that his son was going to win. Daugherty, satisfied with the manner in which he had managed the campaign, left about 10:30 P.M. Warren and Florence Harding stayed on to savor the victory, however, and did not go to bed until 5:00 A.M.

Two hours later, Doctor Harding showed up on the president-elect's lawn in his Grand Army uniform, wearing a gold-corded hat and swinging a stout hickory walking-stick. He received the congratulations of early-morning callers, while his son slept late.

Editors of the *Literary Digest* had sent out millions of postcards in the first poll ever taken during a presidential campaign. From the responses, they concluded that the Republicans would win. However, when the votes were counted, Joseph Tumulty of the *Literary Digest* said, "It wasn't a landslide, it was an earthquake."

Harding had captured a popular vote of 16,152,200, compared to Cox's 9,147,353. The 60-percent win surprised even the Republican leaders. Harding won the electoral vote, 404 to 127. He carried every state outside of the solid South, plus Tennessee. Republican candidates had also won 22 seats in the Senate and 167 in the House of Representatives.

Above: Warren and Florence looking over the election returns on November 6, 1920

Right: Harding with his father, George Tryon Harding II

Harding and his vice-president, Calvin Coolidge

The first people to offer their official congratulations were the members of his own force on the *Marion Daily Star.* They came to the home of their president, their boss, their friend. They presented him with a gold printer's ruler inscribed with the date of his election. The ruler also had a blank space in which they hoped to engrave the record of his reelection in 1924.

As he spoke to these intimate associates, Harding's voice choked and he was unable to control his emotions. With

Florence, Warren, and George Tryon Harding

tears running down his cheeks, he said: "You and I have been associated together for many years. I know you and you know me. I am about to be called to a position of great responsibility. I have been on the square with you and I want to be on the square with all the world."

The newsman from Marion, Ohio, had now achieved the highest position in the America he loved. He would now choose his cabinet members and soon enter the White House as the twenty-ninth president of the United States.

The Harding home in Marion, Ohio, draped with American flags

Right: Harding at work in the composing room of his newspaper, the *Marion Daily Star*

Below: Harding addresses well-wishers from his front porch after his election is confirmed.

Chapter 6

The Harding Cabinet

After a month's vacation in Texas and Panama, President-Elect Harding began choosing his cabinet members, or advisers. He hoped to find men with high qualifications for these positions. Even leading Democrats were called to town to be interviewed. Marion was dubbed "the Great Listening Post."

Already Harding had announced that Calvin Coolidge, his vice-president, would be sitting in on all the cabinet meetings. He was the first vice-president to do this.

On February 19, 1921, the first cabinet appointment was announced. The highly respected Charles Evans Hughes would be the secretary of state. He had been an associate justice of the Supreme Court until 1916, when he resigned to run for the presidency. He lost by a small margin to President Wilson.

Henry C. Wallace was then selected as secretary of agriculture. He had been a farmer and was editor of a farm journal. Herbert H. Hoover was asked to serve as secretary of commerce because he was an engineer and war relief administrator. Multimillionaire banker Andrew W. Mellon became secretary of the treasury. John W. Weeks of Massachusetts, who had served in the Senate with Harding, was selected as secretary of war.

A difficult post to fill was that of secretary of labor. There were many labor disturbances in this postwar period. Finally, James J. Davis of Pennsylvania, who had been a steelworker, was chosen.

Will Hays, who had been chairman of the Republican National Committee, was named postmaster general. Secretary of the Navy would be Edwin Denby, a Detroit lawyer who had made a fortune in the automobile business. He also had been a congressman from Michigan.

The final two selections were to create problems for Harding later. He chose Albert B. Fall out of friendship and Harry M. Daugherty out of gratitude. Fall was also chosen because he had contributed heavily to Harding's campaign.

Fall had an attractive and colorful personality. He had worked in a cotton mill in Nashville, Tennessee, studied law, served as a U.S. marshall in the Texas panhandle, and even prospected for gold in Mexico. During the Spanish-American War he rode with Theodore Roosevelt and his Rough Riders. In 1912 he was elected to the U.S. Senate. It was there, in his broad-brimmed Stetson, flowing black cape, and handlebar mustache, that he had met Harding. Now Harding named him secretary of the interior.

Harry Daugherty was the last one named in the Harding cabinet and was by far the most controversial. It was Daugherty who had convinced Harding to run for the presidency. In fact, Daugherty had been behind many of Harding's political ambitions. Harry Daugherty was Harding's campaign manager and was well versed in practical politics. Now he would be the attorney general.

Harding and cabinet: (Seated, left to right) Weeks, Mellon, Hughes, Harding, Coolidge, Denby; (standing) Fall, Hays, Daugherty, Wallace, Hoover, Davis

As for Daugherty's merits, he was a shrewd lawyer. He had spent many hours as a lobbyist, persuading members of Congress to adopt his political views. Familiar with lobbying tactics, he told a friend, "I know who the crooks are and I want to stand between Harding and them." He was a political troubleshooter. But more important, he was a friend of Harding's, and Harding was angry about the assaults on his friend.

Thus the cabinet was complete. All parts of the country were represented. The men ranged in age from 41 to 65, and their many professions would give balance in future decision making.

An artist's view of the cabinet, from Hughes down to Daugherty

The press finally accepted the Harding choices. As the *New York Times* put it, "From Hughes to Daugherty is a pretty long step." But another writer called it "one of the strongest groups of presidential advisors and department heads in a generation."

Everything was in place now. Harding himself said he wanted to get through the formal ceremonies quickly and without any fuss, so that he might "get his coat off and get to work."

Above: An informal snapshot of Harding and Coolidge
Below: Political cartoons on the Republicans' burdens upon Harding's election

Chapter 7

The Presidency

The inauguration of Warren Gamaliel Harding as president of the United States on March 4, 1921, was described as "the simplest in modern times." Accompanied by outgoing president Woodrow Wilson, he was the first president to ride to his inauguration in an automobile. His front porch in Marion had become famous, so he asked that a small portico resembling the porch be set up on the east steps of the Capitol. There, as a hush came over the crowd, Harding took the oath of office. He was the first president to use a public address system at his inauguration. Because the expenses of the war were still heavy on the American people, it was determined that there would be no inaugural ball and no parade.

His inaugural speech was a talk with the "home folk" who had elected him. He spoke of his great love for America and pleaded for normalcy, unity, and service. He wanted the people of America to know that he was willing to listen to their concerns and make needed changes.

Opposite page: Harding speaks at Plymouth, Massachusetts, in 1921, the 300th anniversary of the Pilgrims' landing.

Above: Harding and Wilson ride in the inaugural carriage.
Below: Crowds assembled for Harding's inauguration ceremony on March 4, 1921

Above: Harding delivers his inaugural address.
Below: The Hardings enter the White House after the inauguration.

Harding believed there were three things that would lead the country back to normalcy. These were to make an immediate peace treaty with Germany, to lower the cost of running the government, and to turn the thoughts of the people toward peacetime production rather than war and destruction.

Almost immediately, Congress took up the question of peace with Germany and passed a resolution declaring the war at an end. Fighting had stopped in November 1918, but no official treaty was signed until August 25, 1921.

With the task of putting life back in order after the war, Allied countries found that the bodies of many soldiers killed in battle could not be identified. Each one of these countries then chose a symbolic unknown soldier, buried his remains near the national capitol, and built a monument in his honor.

On November 11, Armistice Day, America's Unknown Soldier was buried in Arlington National Cemetery near Washington, D.C. President Harding gave an emotional dedication speech at the tomb. He said, "This American soldier went forth to battle with no hatred for any people in the world, but hating war and hating the purpose of every war for conquest."

Then he added, "There must be, there shall be, the commanding voice of a conscious civilization against armed warfare."

Tears ran down the faces of the listeners as they thought of the thousands of American soldiers who had given their lives during World War I and now rested in graves in Europe.

Above: Harding honors the Unknown Soldier at ceremonies in the Capitol rotunda.
Below: Dedication of the tomb of the Unknown Soldier at Arlington National Cemetery

The following day was the beginning of the international Washington Disarmament Conference. Delegates assembled in the Continental Memorial Hall in Washington, D.C. Out of these deliberations came the famous Five-Power Treaty, signed by the United States, Great Britain, France, Italy, and Japan. These nations agreed to limit the number, size, and guns of their battleships for the next fifteen years.

This agreement was the proposal of Secretary of State Charles Evans Hughes. He said that the world was "taking perhaps the greatest forward step in history to establish the reign of peace" because it ended the struggle for naval power.

Harding addressed the delegates on the closing day. "The world," he said, "has hungered for a new assurance of peace in which there would be no victors and no vanquished. This conference has provided it."

Although the treaties signed during this conference were not ratified by the Senate until after Harding's death, the president's reputation as a man of peace was assured in foreign capitals.

Another international matter waiting for the president's action was a treaty with the South American country of Colombia. The treaty had first been presented to the Senate during Wilson's presidency. Now a new treaty was drawn up between the two countries and ratified by the Senate on April 21, 1921. In this treaty, the United States government agreed to pay Colombia $25,000,000 as compensation for its loss of control over Panama and the Panama Canal Zone.

Opposite page: Filling the "peace pipe" with a cut in the size of world navies

Secretary of the Treasury
Andrew W. Mellon

There were also achievements in domestic affairs. Perhaps the most outstanding one was the establishment of a system for preparing a national budget. With Charles G. Dawes as director, the Budget Bureau cut government expenses in three years from six billion dollars to three billion dollars. At the end of 1922, Secretary of the Treasury Mellon announced not only that the budget was balanced, but that there was a surplus of $321,000,000.

The Harding administration helped farmers by giving them more borrowing power. However, it did not meet their demand for lower shipping costs and higher prices.

A serious coal miners' strike was settled during Harding's term. One result of the strike was the appointment of the President's Fact-Finding Commission, which undertook the first official survey of underlying problems in the coal industry.

Three political cartoonists
give their commentaries on
Harding's first year in
the presidency.

Harding appealed to the steel industry to abolish the twelve-hour working day. Steel companies were against this at the time, but shortly after Harding's death they agreed to shorten the workday.

Harding sought to provide hospitalization, vocational training, and monetary compensation for wounded and convalescent soldiers, sailors, and marines. With visions of a great American Merchant Marine, he began his fight for a ship subsidy in 1922.

Harding went into the White House knowing that he faced an enormous task of rebuilding the nation after the war. He spent many long hours behind his desk, arriving by 8:00 A.M. and rarely retiring before midnight.

However, he also took time out for some relaxation. It was said that he had selected a "golf Cabinet." They played on the green at the Chevy Chase Country Club. Harding's average was 101, and he became quite excited when he kept his score in the nineties.

Many of Harding's friends and acquaintances sought jobs and moved to Washington. This group came to be known as the "Ohio Gang," with headquarters at the "Little Green House" at 1625 K Street. Many poker games were played around the tables. Government favors and appointments were bought and sold here, although there is no evidence that Harding himself knew of this.

Sometimes this group of friends attended baseball games with the president. As a child, Warren had played first and third base on an amateur ball team in Marion. This love of baseball continued with him all through his life. Babe Ruth was the great home-run king of the day, and the president watched him play several times in Washington, D.C.

Fishing and yachting were among the sports that the president enjoyed, but he was especially fond of "motoring." He once said, "I have found my cars providers of healthful recreation; extenders and cementers of friendship; and broadeners of acquaintances." Cars were still luxury items in the early 1920s, and President Harding considered driving to be one of his greatest pleasures.

Florence Harding made some changes at the White House, too. The police officers who stood guard at the White House were withdrawn so that the gates could be opened to the general public. She also changed the yard. Thousands of bulbs were planted, and flowers appeared everywhere. Birdhouses were installed in trees.

During the first summer Florence reinstated the White House teas and gave three garden parties. At Christmas, holiday receptions were resumed. Laughter and cheerfulness returned to the White House.

A reception was held on New Year's Day in 1922. Mrs. Harding stood beside the president and shook the hands of over 6,500 people. She told her friends, "My left hand is good for two hours yet!" and held it up—but her right hand had given out. It had to be soaked in hot towels.

One of the First Lady's greatest pleasures was to come down from the upper floor when visitors were roaming about the lower floor. She always extended her hand, smiled, and introduced herself. If not pressed for time, she would walk with them from room to room, pointing out objects of interest as if they were guests in her home.

**Above: Harding golfs at the New Hampshire lodge of Secretary of War Weeks (swinging).
Below: The president taking a relaxing horseback ride through the country**

Above: Harding and Harvey Firestone read as Thomas Edison naps at a country retreat.
Below: Harding (center) on a fishing trip in Florida

Above: Harding with French chemist Madame Marie Curie
Below: Harding with Mrs. and Mrs. Albert Einstein

Above: Baseball fan Harding throws out the first ball in a 1921 game.
Below: Baseball hero Babe Ruth presents a flower to President Harding.

Someone in her hometown who had known her since girlhood gave this description:

"Florence Harding? Oh, she's a fine woman. Nice to everybody. Knows how to run things, too. Runs her house; runs the paper if necessary; runs Warren; runs everything but the car, and could run that if she wanted to. That Florence is all right."

But in 1922, the honeymoon ended. Rumors of corruption, graft, and dishonest dealings began to be heard in Washington. In the congressional elections, Republicans lost seventy House seats and seven Senate seats. Harding felt that the election results reflected a lack of confidence in his administration. However, this loss was probably due to a depression in the economy.

Late in 1922, Harding learned of irregularities in the Veterans' Bureau. The Senate ordered an investigation. Evidence was turned up that the bureau had spent hundreds of millions of dollars for overpriced materials, land sites, and construction. There had been no competitive bidding. Harding was shocked because the head of this bureau was one of his poker-playing friends, Charles R. Forbes. In January 1923, Forbes was allowed to leave on a trip to Europe. Then Harding announced Forbes's resignation and named Brigadier General Frank T. Hines to replace him. In 1924 Forbes was brought to trial for bribery and conspiracy, along with an official of one of the firms with which he had been doing business.

Harding received a second shock in March 1923, with the suicide of Charles F. Cramer, the attorney for the Veterans' Bureau.

Albert Fall (left) and oilman Harry Ford Sinclair during the Teapot Dome hearings

Another close friend, Jesse Smith, left Washington. Unbeknownst to Harding, Smith had been one of the most powerful members in the Ohio Gang for dispensing jobs and favors. Smith returned to Washington a few months later and committed suicide.

There were also rumors of an oil scandal involving Secretary of the Interior Albert Fall. This became known as the "Teapot Dome" affair. Fall had made a crooked business deal with two oil companies. In return for an illegal payment of $400,000, Fall had turned over two valuable tracts of petroleum-rich government land to private companies. They were the Teapot Dome oil reserve in Wyoming and the Elk Hill oil reserve in California. For cheating the government, Fall, together with one oil company executive, was tried and sent to prison in 1931.

Captioned "The Hunter Hunted," this cartoon depicts Daugherty under investigation.

Next, the Senate began an investigation of Attorney General Daugherty to determine why he had not prosecuted the central figures in the oil and Veterans' Bureau scandals. Daugherty was brought to trial twice. Both times, the juries were not able to determine his innocence or guilt. Finally, the case was dropped.

Florence had been ill during much of 1922. Warren became ill with the flu in January 1923, and multiple worries began to affect his health. His golf games exhausted him, and not even poker games could bring the old Warren back. He found it hard to sleep unless he was propped up on a pillow where it was less difficult to breathe.

Finally his physician ordered him to take a vacation as far away as possible from the pressures of Washington.

Harding at his desk

However, Warren felt that this was just a slump in his popularity and that a rise in farm prices and wages would make him popular again. He decided to combine a vacation to Alaska with a speaking tour across the country. He would meet the people face-to-face. Perhaps his presence would help in the disagreements on policies for handling mineral, timber, and fishing rights in Alaska. He could also officiate at the opening of the Alaskan Railway.

As president-elect, Warren Harding had captured the affections of the American people with his winning smile and personality. Now, as president, he would talk with them again. He called this the Journey of Understanding.

Chapter 8

Last Tour of the Peacemaker

On June 20, 1923, President and Mrs. Harding left their pet dog Laddie Boy in Washington, D.C. Together with a few friends and aides, they began their cross-country Journey of Understanding. From the moment they boarded the train, President Harding showed a renewed spirit. His words were inspiring and, as they appeared in the press, even greater throngs of people greeted him. Speaking before large crowds, Harding found a fresh bond of understanding with the American people. He had left the confines of Washington and was among his neighbors once again.

In his speeches, Warren Harding dealt with the practical problems of government and business with a new vision. He spoke not as a party man, but as the friend and neighbor and counselor of all the people.

Though Harding's destination was Alaska, he went through many states giving speeches. His journey took him through West Virginia, Indiana, Illinois, Missouri, Kansas, Colorado, Wyoming, Utah, Idaho, Montana, Oregon, Washington, and on to several cities in Alaska.

Opposite page: President Harding on tour

He spoke on the coal strike in Cheyenne, Wyoming; taxation in Salt Lake City, Utah; prohibition in Denver, Colorado; farm problems in Hutchinson, Kansas; cooperation in Idaho Falls, Idaho; international peace at Helena, Montana; conservation at Spokane, Washington; and restriction of immigration in Portland, Oregon.

From city to city, village to village, Harding spoke to huge audiences in auditoriums and to smaller groups from the platform of his railroad car. His visit to Vancouver, British Columbia, was significant. It was the first time that a president of the United States had visited Canada, and the people gave him an enthusiastic greeting.

On July 27, President Harding spoke in Seattle, Washington. It was his last public address, for during this visit he became ill. Aides tried to persuade him to abandon the rest of the trip, but Harding insisted they continue on to San Francisco.

A great welcome had been planned there for the chief executive, but when word arrived of his sudden illness, rejoicing turned to concern. President Harding now complained of indigestion and showed signs of bronchial pneumonia. By the time he arrived in San Francisco on July 29, it was clear that all speech-making engagements would have to be canceled.

News reports on his condition were extremely serious for a day or two; then came reassuring bulletins. Hopes began to rise. On Thursday, August 2, it was reported that "the President had several hours of restful sleep during the night and except for marked exhaustion by an acute illness, expressed himself as feeling easier this morning."

Above: President and Mrs. Harding view a fish catch in Alaska.
Below: The last photo taken of Harding, as he leaves his train in San Francisco

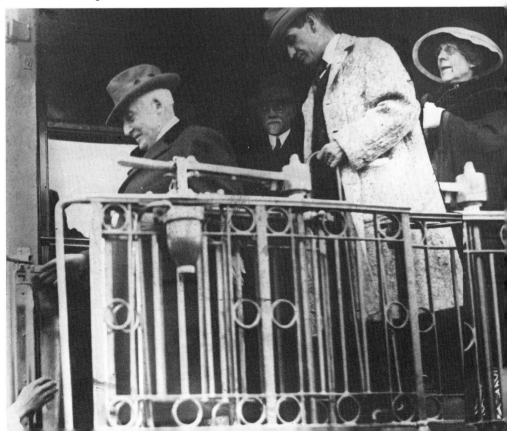

The doctor was so satisfied with the day's progress that he went for an automobile ride. Two little girls came to the presidential suite just before seven o'clock, and Mrs. Harding accepted their gift of flowers. She went back to the room and started reading to the president. When she stopped, he said, "That's good. Go on, read some more." Those were his last words.

It was 7:30 on Thursday evening, August 2, 1923. A shudder ran through his body and he collapsed. The doctors could do nothing. The president was dead.

The shock to the nation was profound. Across the country, flags were lowered to half-staff. President Harding's body was placed in a funeral train and moved eastward to Washington. Some three million persons crowded the tracks to watch the funeral train, draped with a black flag, pass by.

A newspaper reporter described the funeral train's trip this way:

"They gathered from factory and farm, from unpainted hut and mansion. The farmer boy paused at his work in the hayfield to doff his hat to the funeral train bearing the body of a President who had begun life on the farm. At the crossroads were merchants and laborers. Housekeeper and maid stood on the porch together. One touch of nature had made the whole world kin. The windows and roofs of the factories were filled with men and women, employers and employed, reverently hushed. The veterans of old wars and new stood side by side in salutation of the Commander-in-chief for whom the flags were everywhere half-masted."

Harding's body lying in state in the rotunda

The train reached Washington shortly before midnight on Tuesday, August 7. Harding's body was taken to the East Room of the White House and then into the spacious rotunda, where people could pay tribute to his memory.

Finally the body was taken by train back to his home in Marion, Ohio. After two years and five months in office, Warren Gamaliel Harding was back with the "home folks." As he lay in state at his father's home, people visited all through the afternoon, all through the night, and through the morning hours until the funeral.

On Friday, August 10, funeral services were held and the casket placed into a vault. He was gone, but his smile was remembered by every American. The general public had not yet heard of the scandals brought about by greedy and unfaithful friends. They only mourned the loss of their beloved friend and president.

The Harding Memorial in Marion, Ohio

Florence Harding died fifteen months later. Her remains were placed next to Warren's in the beautiful Harding Memorial at Marion, Ohio.

To the best of his ability, Warren Harding had served the people of the United States and the world. Above all, he had had faith in America. In his acceptance speech of July 22, 1920, he had summed it all up: "Whether enemies threaten from without or menaces arise from within, there is some indefinable voice saying, 'Have confidence in the Republic! America will go on!'"

Chronology of American History

(Shaded area covers events in Warren G. Harding's lifetime.)

About A.D. 982—Eric the Red, born in Norway, reaches Greenland in one of the first European voyages to North America.

About 1000—Leif Ericson (Eric the Red's son) leads what is thought to be the first European expedition to mainland North America; Leif probably lands in Canada.

1492—Christopher Columbus, seeking a sea route from Spain to the Far East, discovers the New World.

1497—John Cabot reaches Canada in the first English voyage to North America.

1513—Ponce de Léon explores Florida in search of the fabled Fountain of Youth.

1519-1521—Hernando Cortés of Spain conquers Mexico.

1534—French explorers led by Jacques Cartier enter the Gulf of St. Lawrence in Canada.

1540—Spanish explorer Francisco Coronado begins exploring the American Southwest, seeking the riches of the mythical Seven Cities of Cibola.

1565—St. Augustine, Florida, the first permanent European town in what is now the United States, is founded by the Spanish.

1607—Jamestown, Virginia, is founded, the first permanent English town in the present-day U.S.

1608—Frenchman Samuel de Champlain founds the village of Quebec, Canada.

1609—Henry Hudson explores the eastern coast of present-day U.S. for the Netherlands; the Dutch then claim parts of New York, New Jersey, Delaware, and Connecticut and name the area New Netherland.

1619—The English colonies' first shipment of black slaves arrives in Jamestown.

1620—English Pilgrims found Massachusetts' first permanent town at Plymouth.

1621—Massachusetts Pilgrims and Indians hold the famous first Thanksgiving feast in colonial America.

1623—Colonization of New Hampshire is begun by the English.

1624—Colonization of present-day New York State is begun by the Dutch at Fort Orange (Albany).

1625—The Dutch start building New Amsterdam (now New York City).

1630—The town of Boston, Massachusetts, is founded by the English Puritans.

1633—Colonization of Connecticut is begun by the English.

1634—Colonization of Maryland is begun by the English.

1636—Harvard, the colonies' first college, is founded in Massachusetts. Rhode Island colonization begins when Englishman Roger Williams founds Providence.

1638—Delaware colonization begins as Swedes build Fort Christina at present-day Wilmington.

1640—Stephen Daye of Cambridge, Massachusetts prints *The Bay Psalm Book*, the first English-language book published in what is now the U.S.

1643—Swedish settlers begin colonizing Pennsylvania.

About 1650—North Carolina is colonized by Virginia settlers.

1660—New Jersey colonization is begun by the Dutch at present-day Jersey City.

1670—South Carolina colonization is begun by the English near Charleston.

1673—Jacques Marquette and Louis Jolliet explore the upper Mississippi River for France.

1682—Philadelphia, Pennsylvania, is settled. La Salle explores Mississippi River all the way to its mouth in Louisiana and claims the whole Mississippi Valley for France.

1693—College of William and Mary is founded in Williamsburg, Virginia.

1700—Colonial population is about 250,000.

1703—Benjamin Franklin is born in Boston.

1732—George Washington, first president of the U.S., is born in Westmoreland County, Virginia.

1733—James Oglethorpe founds Savannah, Georgia; Georgia is established as the thirteenth colony.

1735—John Adams, second president of the U.S., is born in Braintree, Massachusetts.

1737—William Byrd founds Richmond, Virginia.

1738—British troops are sent to Georgia over border dispute with Spain.

1739—Black insurrection takes place in South Carolina.

1740—English Parliament passes act allowing naturalization of immigrants to American colonies after seven-year residence.

1743—Thomas Jefferson is born in Albemarle County, Virginia. Benjamin Franklin retires at age thirty-seven to devote himself to scientific inquiries and public service.

1744—King George's War begins; France joins war effort against England.

1745—During King George's War, France raids settlements in Maine and New York.

1747—Classes begin at Princeton College in New Jersey.

1748—The Treaty of Aix-la-Chapelle concludes King George's War.

1749—Parliament legally recognizes slavery in colonies and the inauguration of the plantation system in the South. George Washington becomes the surveyor for Culpepper County in Virginia.

1750—Thomas Walker passes through and names Cumberland Gap on his way toward Kentucky region. Colonial population is about 1,200,000.

1751—James Madison, fourth president of the U.S., is born in Port Conway, Virginia. English Parliament passes Currency Act, banning New England colonies from issuing paper money. George Washington travels to Barbados.

1752—Pennsylvania Hospital, the first general hospital in the colonies, is founded in Philadelphia. Benjamin Franklin uses a kite in a thunderstorm to demonstrate that lightning is a form of electricity.

1753—George Washington delivers command that the French withdraw from the Ohio River Valley; French disregard the demand. Colonial population is about 1,328,000.

1754—French and Indian War begins (extends to Europe as the Seven Years' War). Washington surrenders at Fort Necessity.

1755—French and Indians ambush Braddock. Washington becomes commander of Virginia troops.

1756—England declares war on France.

1758—James Monroe, fifth president of the U.S., is born in Westmoreland County, Virginia.

1759—Cherokee Indian war begins in southern colonies; hostilities extend to 1761. George Washington marries Martha Dandridge Custis.

1760—George III becomes king of England. Colonial population is about 1,600,000.

1762—England declares war on Spain.

1763—Treaty of Paris concludes the French and Indian War and the Seven Years' War. England gains Canada and most other French lands east of the Mississippi River.

1764—British pass the Sugar Act to gain tax money from the colonists. The issue of taxation without representation is first introduced in Boston. John Adams marries Abigail Smith.

1765—Stamp Act goes into effect in the colonies. Business virtually stops as almost all colonists refuse to use the stamps.

1766—British repeal the Stamp Act.

1767—John Quincy Adams, sixth president of the U.S. and son of second president John Adams, is born in Braintree, Massachusetts. Andrew Jackson, seventh president of the U.S., is born in Waxhaw settlement, South Carolina.

1769—Daniel Boone sights the Kentucky Territory.

1770—In the Boston Massacre, British soldiers kill five colonists and injure six. Townshend Acts are repealed, thus eliminating all duties on imports to the colonies except tea.

1771—Benjamin Franklin begins his autobiography, a work that he will never complete. The North Carolina assembly passes the "Bloody Act," which makes rioters guilty of treason.

1772—Samuel Adams rouses colonists to consider British threats to self-government.

1773—English Parliament passes the Tea Act. Colonists dressed as Mohawk Indians board British tea ships and toss 342 casks of tea into the water in what becomes known as the Boston Tea Party. William Henry Harrison is born in Charles City County, Virginia.

1774—British close the port of Boston to punish the city for the Boston Tea Party. First Continental Congress convenes in Philadelphia.

1775—American Revolution begins with battles of Lexington and Concord, Massachusetts. Second Continental Congress opens in Philadelphia. George Washington becomes commander-in-chief of the Continental army.

1776—Declaration of Independence is adopted on July 4.

1777—Congress adopts the American flag with thirteen stars and thirteen stripes. John Adams is sent to France to negotiate peace treaty.

1778—France declares war against Great Britain and becomes U.S. ally.

1779—British surrender to Americans at Vincennes. Thomas Jefferson is elected governor of Virginia. James Madison is elected to the Continental Congress.

1780—Benedict Arnold, first American traitor, defects to the British.

1781—Articles of Confederation go into effect. Cornwallis surrenders to George Washington at Yorktown, ending the American Revolution.

1782—American commissioners, including John Adams, sign peace treaty with British in Paris. Thomas Jefferson's wife, Martha, dies. Martin Van Buren is born in Kinderhook, New York.

1784—Zachary Taylor is born near Barboursville, Virginia.

1785—Congress adopts the dollar as the unit of currency. John Adams is made minister to Great Britain. Thomas Jefferson is appointed minister to France.

1786—Shays's Rebellion begins in Massachusetts.

1787—Constitutional Convention assembles in Philadelphia, with George Washington presiding; U.S. Constitution is adopted. Delaware, New Jersey, and Pennsylvania become states.

1788—Virginia, South Carolina, New York, Connecticut, New Hampshire, Maryland, and Massachusetts become states. U.S. Constitution is ratified. New York City is declared U.S. capital.

1789—Presidential electors elect George Washington and John Adams as first president and vice-president. Thomas Jefferson is appointed secretary of state. North Carolina becomes a state. French Revolution begins.

1790—Supreme Court meets for the first time. Rhode Island becomes a state. First national census in the U.S. counts 3,929,214 persons. John Tyler is born in Charles City County, Virginia.

1791—Vermont enters the Union. U.S. Bill of Rights, the first ten amendments to the Constitution, goes into effect. District of Columbia is established. James Buchanan is born in Stony Batter, Pennsylvania.

1792—Thomas Paine publishes *The Rights of Man*. Kentucky becomes a state. Two political parties are formed in the U.S., Federalist and Republican. Washington is elected to a second term, with Adams as vice-president.

1793—War between France and Britain begins; U.S. declares neutrality. Eli Whitney invents the cotton gin; cotton production and slave labor increase in the South.

1794—Eleventh Amendment to the Constitution is passed, limiting federal courts' power. "Whiskey Rebellion" in Pennsylvania protests federal whiskey tax. James Madison marries Dolley Payne Todd.

1795—George Washington signs the Jay Treaty with Great Britain. Treaty of San Lorenzo, between U.S. and Spain, settles Florida boundary and gives U.S. right to navigate the Mississippi. James Polk is born near Pineville, North Carolina.

1796—Tennessee enters the Union. Washington gives his Farewell Address, refusing a third presidential term. John Adams is elected president and Thomas Jefferson vice-president.

1797—Adams recommends defense measures against possible war with France. Napoleon Bonaparte and his army march against Austrians in Italy. U.S. population is about 4,900,000.

1798—Washington is named commander-in-chief of the U.S. Army. Department of the Navy is created. Alien and Sedition Acts are passed. Napoleon's troops invade Egypt and Switzerland.

1799—George Washington dies at Mount Vernon, New York. James Monroe is elected governor of Virginia. French Revolution ends. Napoleon becomes ruler of France.

1800—Thomas Jefferson and Aaron Burr tie for president. U.S. capital is moved from Philadelphia to Washington, D.C. The White House is built as presidents' home. Spain returns Louisiana to France. Millard Fillmore is born in Locke, New York.

1801—After thirty-six ballots, House of Representatives elects Thomas Jefferson president, making Burr vice-president. James Madison is named secretary of state.

1802—Congress abolishes excise taxes. U.S. Military Academy is founded at West Point, New York.

1803—Ohio enters the Union. Louisiana Purchase treaty is signed with France, greatly expanding U.S. territory.

1804—Twelfth Amendment to the Constitution rules that president and vice-president be elected separately. Alexander Hamilton is killed by Vice-President Aaron Burr in a duel. Orleans Territory is established. Napoleon crowns himself emperor of France. Franklin Pierce is born in Hillsborough Lower Village, New Hampshire.

1805—Thomas Jefferson begins his second term as president. Lewis and Clark expedition reaches the Pacific Ocean.

1806—Coinage of silver dollars is stopped; resumes in 1836.

1807—Aaron Burr is acquitted in treason trial. Embargo Act closes U.S. ports to trade.

1808—James Madison is elected president. Congress outlaws importing slaves from Africa. Andrew Johnson is born in Raleigh, North Carolina.

1809—Abraham Lincoln is born near Hodgenville, Kentucky.

1810—U.S. population is 7,240,000.

1811—William Henry Harrison defeats Indians at Tippecanoe. Monroe is named secretary of state.

1812—Louisiana becomes a state. U.S. declares war on Britain (War of 1812). James Madison is reelected president. Napoleon invades Russia.

1813—British forces take Fort Niagara and Buffalo, New York.

1814—Francis Scott Key writes "The Star-Spangled Banner." British troops burn much of Washington, D.C., including the White House. Treaty of Ghent ends War of 1812. James Monroe becomes secretary of war.

1815—Napoleon meets his final defeat at Battle of Waterloo.

1816—James Monroe is elected president. Indiana becomes a state.

1817—Mississippi becomes a state. Construction on Erie Canal begins.

1818—Illinois enters the Union. The present thirteen-stripe flag is adopted. Border between U.S. and Canada is agreed upon.

1819—Alabama becomes a state. U.S. purchases Florida from Spain. Thomas Jefferson establishes the University of Virginia.

1820—James Monroe is reelected. In the Missouri Compromise, Maine enters the Union as a free (non-slave) state.

1821—Missouri enters the Union as a slave state. Santa Fe Trail opens the American Southwest. Mexico declares independence from Spain. Napoleon Bonaparte dies.

1822—U.S. recognizes Mexico and Colombia. Liberia in Africa is founded as a home for freed slaves. Ulysses S. Grant is born in Point Pleasant, Ohio. Rutherford B. Hayes is born in Delaware, Ohio.

1823—Monroe Doctrine closes North and South America to European colonizing or invasion.

1824—House of Representatives elects John Quincy Adams president when none of the four candidates wins a majority in national election. Mexico becomes a republic.

1825—Erie Canal is opened. U.S. population is 11,300,000.

1826—Thomas Jefferson and John Adams both die on July 4, the fiftieth anniversary of the Declaration of Independence.

1828—Andrew Jackson is elected president. Tariff of Abominations is passed, cutting imports.

1829—James Madison attends Virginia's constitutional convention. Slavery is abolished in Mexico. Chester A. Arthur is born in Fairfield, Vermont.

1830—Indian Removal Act to resettle Indians west of the Mississippi is approved.

1831—James Monroe dies in New York City. James A. Garfield is born in Orange, Ohio. Cyrus McCormick develops his reaper.

1832—Andrew Jackson, nominated by the new Democratic Party, is reelected president.

1833—Britain abolishes slavery in its colonies. Benjamin Harrison is born in North Bend, Ohio.

1835—Federal government becomes debt-free for the first time.

1836—Martin Van Buren becomes president. Texas wins independence from Mexico. Arkansas joins the Union. James Madison dies at Montpelier, Virginia.

1837—Michigan enters the Union. U.S. population is 15,900,000. Grover Cleveland is born in Caldwell, New Jersey.

1840—William Henry Harrison is elected president.

1841—President Harrison dies in Washington, D.C., one month after inauguration. Vice-President John Tyler succeeds him.

1843—William McKinley is born in Niles, Ohio.

1844—James Knox Polk is elected president. Samuel Morse sends first telegraphic message.

1845—Texas and Florida become states. Potato famine in Ireland causes massive emigration from Ireland to U.S. Andrew Jackson dies near Nashville, Tennessee.

1846—Iowa enters the Union. War with Mexico begins.

1847—U.S. captures Mexico City.

1848—Zachary Taylor becomes president. Treaty of Guadalupe Hidalgo ends Mexico-U.S. war. Wisconsin becomes a state.

1849—James Polk dies in Nashville, Tennessee.

1850—President Taylor dies in Washington, D.C.; Vice-President Millard Fillmore succeeds him. California enters the Union, breaking tie between slave and free states.

1852—Franklin Pierce is elected president.

1853—Gadsden Purchase transfers Mexican territory to U.S.

1854—"War for Bleeding Kansas" is fought between slave and free states.

1855—Czar Nicholas I of Russia dies, succeeded by Alexander II.

1856—James Buchanan is elected pleasant. In Massacre of Potawatomi Creek, Kansas-slavers are murdered by free-staters. Woodrow Wilson is born in Staunton, Pennsylvania.

1857—William Howard Taft is born in Cincinnati, Ohio.

1858—Minnesota enters the Union. Theodore Roosevelt is born in New York City.

1859—Oregon becomes a state.

1860—Abraham Lincoln is elected president; South Carolina secedes from the Union in protest.

1861—Arkansas, Tennessee, North Carolina, and Virginia secede. Kansas enters the Union as a free state. Civil War begins.

1862—Union forces capture Fort Henry, Roanoke Island, Fort Donelson, Jacksonville, and New Orleans; Union armies are defeated at the battles of Bull Run and Fredericksburg. Martin Van Buren dies in Kinderhook, New York. John Tyler dies near Charles City, Virginia.

1863—Lincoln issues Emancipation Proclamation: all slaves held in rebelling territories are declared free. West Virginia becomes a state.

1864—Abraham Lincoln is reelected. Nevada becomes a state.

1865—Lincoln is assassinated in Washington, D.C., and succeeded by Andrew Johnson. U.S. Civil War ends on May 26. Thirteenth Amendment abolishes slavery. Warren G. Harding is born in Blooming Grove, Ohio.

1867—Nebraska becomes a state. U.S. buys Alaska from Russia for $7,200,000. Reconstruction Acts are passed.

1868—President Johnson is impeached for violating Tenure of Office Act, but is acquitted by Senate. Ulysses S. Grant is elected president. Fourteenth Amendment prohibits voting discrimination. James Buchanan dies in Lancaster, Pennsylvania.

1869—Franklin Pierce dies in Concord, New Hampshire.

1870—Fifteenth Amendment gives blacks the right to vote.

1872—Grant is reelected over Horace Greeley. General Amnesty Act pardons ex-Confederates. Calvin Coolidge is born in Plymouth Notch, Vermont.

1874—Millard Fillmore dies in Buffalo, New York. Herbert Hoover is born in West Branch, Iowa.

1875—Andrew Johnson dies in Carter's Station, Tennessee.

1876—Colorado enters the Union. "Custer's last stand": he and his men are massacred by Sioux Indians at Little Big Horn, Montana.

1877—Rutherford B. Hayes is elected president as all disputed votes are awarded to him.

1880—James A. Garfield is elected president.

1881—President Garfield is assassinated and dies in Elberon, New Jersey. Vice-President Chester A. Arthur succeeds him.

1882—U.S. bans Chinese immigration. Franklin D. Roosevelt is born in Hyde Park, New York.

1885—Ulysses S. Grant dies in Mount McGregor, New York.

1886—Statue of Liberty is dedicated. Chester A. Arthur dies in New York City.

1888—Benjamin Harrison is elected president.

1889—North Dakota, South Dakota, Washington, and Montana become states.

1890—Dwight D. Eisenhower is born in Denison, Texas. Idaho and Wyoming become states.

1892—Grover Cleveland is elected president.

1893—Rutherford B. Hayes dies in Fremont, Ohio.

1896—William McKinley is elected president. Utah becomes a state.

1898—U.S. declares war on Spain over Cuba.

1899—Philippines demand independence from U.S.

1900—McKinley is reelected. Boxer Rebellion against foreigners in China begins.

1901—McKinley is assassinated by anarchist Leon Czolgosz in Buffalo, New York; Theodore Roosevelt becomes president. Benjamin Harrison dies in Indianapolis, Indiana.

1902—U.S. acquires perpetual control over Panama Canal.

1903—Alaskan frontier is settled.

1904—Russian-Japanese War breaks out. Theodore Roosevelt wins presidential election.

1905—Treaty of Portsmouth signed, ending Russian-Japanese War.

1906—U.S. troops occupy Cuba.

1907—President Roosevelt bars all Japanese immigration. Oklahoma enters the Union.

1908—William Howard Taft becomes president. Grover Cleveland dies in Princeton, New Jersey. Lyndon B. Johnson is born near Stonewall, Texas.

1909—NAACP is founded under W.E.B. DuBois

1910—China abolishes slavery.

1911—Chinese Revolution begins. Ronald Reagan is born in Tampico, Illinois.

1912—Woodrow Wilson is elected president. Arizona and New Mexico become states.

1913—Federal income tax is introduced in U.S. through the Sixteenth Amendment. Richard Nixon is born in Yorba Linda, California. Gerald Ford is born in Omaha, Nebraska.

1914—World War I begins.

1915—British liner *Lusitania* is sunk by German submarine.

1916—Wilson is reelected president.

1917—U.S. breaks diplomatic relations with Germany. Czar Nicholas of Russia abdicates as revolution begins. U.S. declares war on Austria-Hungary. John F. Kennedy is born in Brookline, Massachusetts.

1918—Wilson proclaims "Fourteen Points" as war aims. On November 11, armistice is signed between Allies and Germany.

1919—Eighteenth Amendment prohibits sale and manufacture of intoxicating liquors. Wilson presides over first League of Nations; wins Nobel Peace Prize. Theodore Roosevelt dies in Oyster Bay, New York.

1920—Nineteenth Amendment (women's suffrage) is passed. Warren Harding is elected president.

1921—Adolf Hitler's stormtroopers begin to terrorize political opponents.

1922—Irish Free State is established. Soviet states form USSR. Benito Mussolini forms Fascist government in Italy.

1923—President Harding dies in San Francisco, California; he is succeeded by Vice-President Calvin Coolidge.

1924—Coolidge is elected president. Woodrow Wilson dies in Washington, D.C. James Carter is born in Plains, Georgia. George Bush is born in Milton, Massachusetts.

1925—Hitler reorganizes Nazi Party and publishes first volume of *Mein Kampf.*

1926—Fascist youth organizations founded in Germany and Italy. Republic of Lebanon proclaimed.

1927—Stalin becomes Soviet dictator. Economic conference in Geneva attended by fifty-two nations.

1928—Herbert Hoover is elected president. U.S. and many other nations sign Kellogg-Briand pacts to outlaw war.

1929—Stock prices in New York crash on "Black Thursday"; the Great Depression begins.

1930—Bank of U.S. and its many branches close (most significant bank failure of the year). William Howard Taft dies in Washington, D.C.

1931—Emigration from U.S. exceeds immigration for first time as Depression deepens.

1932—Franklin D. Roosevelt wins presidential election in a Democratic landslide.

1933—First concentration camps are erected in Germany. U.S. recognizes USSR and resumes trade. Twenty-First Amendment repeals prohibition. Calvin Coolidge dies in Northampton, Massachusetts.

1934—Severe dust storms hit Plains states. President Roosevelt passes U.S. Social Security Act.

1936—Roosevelt is reelected. Spanish Civil War begins. Hitler and Mussolini form Rome-Berlin Axis.

1937—Roosevelt signs Neutrality Act.

1938—Roosevelt sends appeal to Hitler and Mussolini to settle European problems amicably.

1939—Germany takes over Czechoslovakia and invades Poland, starting World War II.

1940—Roosevelt is reelected for a third term.

1941—Japan bombs Pearl Harbor, U.S. declares war on Japan. Germany and Italy declare war on U.S.; U.S. then declares war on them.

1942—Allies agree not to make separate peace treaties with the enemies. U.S. government transfers more than 100,000 Nisei (Japanese-Americans) from west coast to inland concentration camps.

1943—Allied bombings of Germany begin.

1944—Roosevelt is reelected for a fourth term. Allied forces invade Normandy on D-Day.

1945—President Franklin D. Roosevelt dies in Warm Springs, Georgia; Vice-President Harry S. Truman succeeds him. Mussolini is killed; Hitler commits suicide. Germany surrenders. U.S. drops atomic bomb on Hiroshima; Japan surrenders: end of World War II.

1946—U.N. General Assembly holds its first session in London. Peace conference of twenty-one nations is held in Paris.

1947—Peace treaties are signed in Paris. "Cold War" is in full swing.

1948—U.S. passes Marshall Plan Act, providing $17 billion in aid for Europe. U.S. recognizes new nation of Israel. India and Pakistan become free of British rule. Truman is elected president.

1949—Republic of Eire is proclaimed in Dublin. Russia blocks land route access from Western Germany to Berlin; airlift begins. U.S., France, and Britain agree to merge their zones of occupation in West Germany. Apartheid program begins in South Africa.

1950—Riots in Johannesburg, South Africa, against apartheid. North Korea invades South Korea. U.N. forces land in South Korea and recapture Seoul.

1951—Twenty-Second Amendment limits president to two terms.

1952—Dwight D. Eisenhower resigns as supreme commander in Europe and is elected president.

1953—Stalin dies; struggle for power in Russia follows. Rosenbergs are executed for espionage.

1954—U.S. and Japan sign mutual defense agreement.

1955—Blacks in Montgomery, Alabama, boycott segregated bus lines.

1956—Eisenhower is reelected president. Soviet troops march into Hungary.

1957—U.S. agrees to withdraw ground forces from Japan. Russia launches first satellite, *Sputnik*.

1958—European Common Market comes into being. Alaska becomes the forty-ninth state. Fidel Castro begins war against Batista government in Cuba.

1959—Hawaii becomes fiftieth state. Castro becomes premier of Cuba. De Gaulle is proclaimed president of the Fifth Republic of France.

1960—Historic debates between Senator John F. Kennedy and Vice-President Richard Nixon are televised. Kennedy is elected president. Brezhnev becomes president of USSR.

1961—Berlin Wall is constructed. Kennedy and Khrushchev confer in Vienna. In Bay of Pigs incident, Cubans trained by CIA attempt to overthrow Castro.

1962—U.S. military council is established in South Vietnam.

1963—Riots and beatings by police and whites mark civil rights demonstrations in Birmingham, Alabama; 30,000 troops are called out, Martin Luther King, Jr., is arrested. Freedom marchers descend on Washington, D.C., to demonstrate. President Kennedy is assassinated in Dallas, Texas; Vice-President Lyndon B. Johnson is sworn in as president.

1964—U.S. aircraft bomb North Vietnam. Johnson is elected president. Herbert Hoover dies in New York City.

1965—U.S. combat troops arrive in South Vietnam.

1966—Thousands protest U.S. policy in Vietnam. National Guard quells race riots in Chicago.

1967—Six-Day War between Israel and Arab nations.

1968—Martin Luther King, Jr., is assassinated in Memphis, Tennessee. Senator Robert Kennedy is assassinated in Los Angeles. Riots and police brutality take place at Democratic National Convention in Chicago. Richard Nixon is elected president. Czechoslovakia is invaded by Soviet troops.

1969—Dwight D. Eisenhower dies in Washington, D.C. Hundreds of thousands of people in several U.S. cities demonstrate against Vietnam War.

1970—Four Vietnam War protesters are killed by National Guardsmen at Kent State University in Ohio.

1971—Twenty-Sixth Amendment allows eighteen-year-olds to vote.

1972—Nixon visits Communist China; is reelected president in near-record landslide. Watergate affair begins when five men are arrested in the Watergate hotel complex in Washington, D.C. Nixon announces resignations of aides Haldeman, Ehrlichman, and Dean and Attorney General Kleindienst as a result of Watergate-related charges. Harry S. Truman dies in Kansas City, Missouri.

1973—Vice-President Spiro Agnew resigns; Gerald Ford is named vice-president. Vietnam peace treaty is formally approved after nineteen months of negotiations. Lyndon B. Johnson dies in San Antonio, Texas.

1974—As a result of Watergate cover-up, impeachment is considered; Nixon resigns and Ford becomes president. Ford pardons Nixon and grants limited amnesty to Vietnam War draft evaders and military deserters.

1975—U.S. civilians are evacuated from Saigon, South Vietnam, as Communist forces complete takeover of South Vietnam.

1976—U.S. celebrates its Bicentennial. James Earl Carter becomes president.

1977—Carter pardons most Vietnam draft evaders, numbering some 10,000.

1980—Ronald Reagan is elected president.

1981—President Reagan is shot in the chest in assassination attempt. Sandra Day O'Connor is appointed first woman justice of the Supreme Court.

1983—U.S. troops invade island of Grenada.

1984—Reagan is reelected president. Democratic candidate Walter Mondale's running mate, Geraldine Ferraro, is the first woman selected for vice-president by a major U.S. political party.

1985—Soviet Communist Party secretary Konstantin Chernenko dies; Mikhail Gorbachev succeeds him. U.S. and Soviet officials discuss arms control in Geneva. Reagan and Gorbachev hold summit conference in Geneva. Racial tensions accelerate in South Africa.

1986—Space shuttle *Challenger* explodes shortly after takeoff; crew of seven dies. U.S. bombs bases in Libya. Corazon Aquino defeats Ferdinand Marcos in Philippine presidential election.

1987—Iraqi missile rips the U.S. frigate *Stark* in the Persian Gulf, killing thirty-seven American sailors. Congress holds hearings to investigate sale of U.S. arms to Iran to finance Nicaraguan *contra* movement.

1988—George Bush is elected president. President Reagan and Soviet leader Gorbachev sign INF treaty, eliminating intermediate nuclear forces. Severe drought sweeps the United States.

1989—East Germany opens Berlin Wall, allowing citizens free exit. Communists lose control of governments in Poland, Rumania, and Czechoslovakia. Chinese troops massacre over 1,000 pro-democracy student demonstrators in Beijing's Tiananmen Square.

Index

Page numbers in boldface type indicate illustrations.

About the Author

Linda R. Wade is a school librarian and free-lance writer living in Fort Wayne, Indiana. Her work has appeared in a number of journals and other publications. As an instructor and lecturer, she has contributed to many writers' conferences and workshops. Ms. Wade's position as a media specialist in an elementary school library has enriched her interest in, and love for, children's literature.

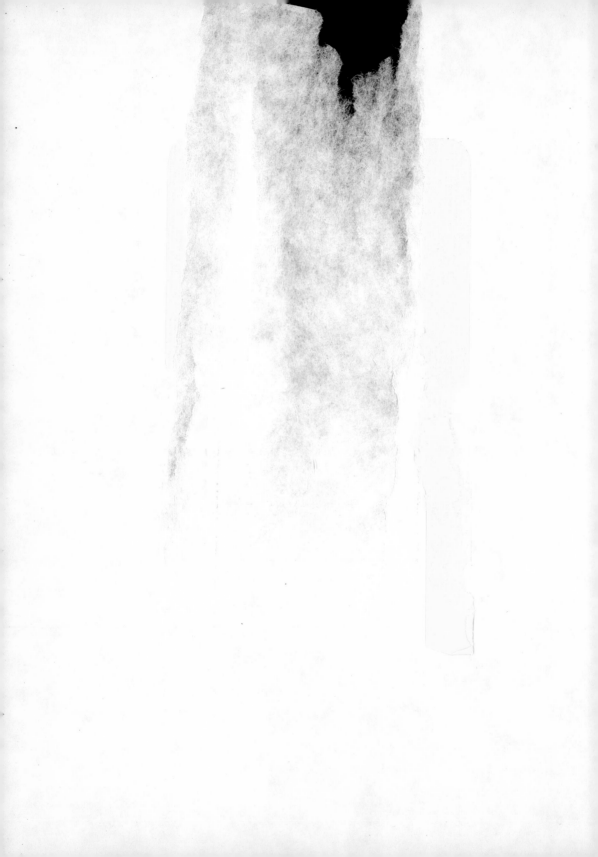